Nancy KERRIGAN

Courageous Skater

Written and Illustrated by Jim Spence

THE ROURKE PRESS, INC.
VERO BEACH, FL 32964

Edited by Sandra A. Robinson and Pamela J.P. Schroeder

LIBRARY OF CONGRESS CATALOGING-IN-PUBLICATION DATA

Spence, Jim.
    Nancy Kerrigan, the courageous skater / written and illustrated by
Jim Spence.
        p. cm. — (Great comeback champions)
    Summary: Relates the series of championships leading up to the
1994 Olympic medal which this small town girl won after having
overcome a knee injury.
    ISBN 1-57103-008-5
    1. Kerrigan, Nancy, 1969-   —Juvenile literature. 2. Women
skaters—United States—Biography—Juvenile literature. [1. Kerrigan,
Nancy, 1969- . 2. Ice skaters. 3. Women—Biography.] I. Title.
II. Series: Spence, Jim. Great comeback champions.
GV850.K38S64 1995
796.91'2'092—dc20
[B]   95-5362
                                                CIP
                                                AC

Printed in the USA

The figure glides across the ice like a swan on a lake. "What a beautiful, flawless display of skating, ladies and gentlemen," the TV announcer says excitedly. "Nancy Kerrigan has shown the world she has a heart filled with courage."

Growing Up

Nancy Kerrigan grew up in the small town of
Stoneham, Massachusetts. Her father supported the
family by working as a welder. When Nancy was only
one year old, her mother developed a rare virus in both
her eyes, and almost lost all of her sight. Throughout
Nancy's skating career, her mom had to look very
closely at a TV screen to see her daughter skate.

Nancy was very athletic, even as a child. She was always interested in learning new things. Her parents took her to ballet class, and she took skiing and swimming lessons, too.

Starting Out

Another sport Nancy liked was figure skating. She
began to take lessons with other girls at the
Stoneham Ice Arena. By the time she was eight,
Nancy's talent as a skater began to stand out. She
could already perform difficult moves while gliding
gracefully across the ice. In 1979, 10-year-old Nancy
Kerrigan entered her first competitive skating match,
the Boston Open. Nancy won second place!

   Soon everyone in Stoneham knew about the little
girl who could skate so beautifully. Throughout her
teenage years, Nancy brought home more trophies
and more medals. Nancy's parents were very proud of
her, and they began to realize their daughter could
one day be an Olympic star.

Sometimes Nancy's skating meets were far away, and she had to take time off from school to travel. However, her teachers found her to be a very good student who worked hard and always made up her work.

In 1992, Nancy was ready to enter her most important skating event yet, the United States Nationals. If she placed well, she would qualify for the Olympic team. Nancy skated beautifully and won the silver medal. Now she would represent the United States in the 1992 Olympic Winter Games!

9

WELCOME HOME NANCY KERRIGAN

Living Her Dream

The 1992 Olympics were held in Albertville, France. Nancy's parents were there to cheer her on. Nancy wanted to skate well. She amazed everyone when she took third place, winning the bronze medal in her first Olympic competition!

When Nancy returned home, the whole town of Stoneham held a party in her honor. It was called "Welcome Home Nancy Kerrigan Day" and was celebrated with a parade, speeches and music. At night Nancy demonstrated her winning style in an ice show held for her community. Nancy had a lot of fun and was looking forward to the next Olympic Winter Games.

Facing a Setback

In 1994, Nancy once again had to qualify for the Olympic team by entering the U.S. Nationals. The Nationals were in Detroit's Cobo Hall, and Nancy was at the rink early to practice her routine.

Moments after she stepped off the ice, something terrible happened. A strange man ran by and struck Nancy across the knee with a club. As Nancy cried out in pain, she wondered why someone would do such a horrible thing. Soon the world would hear the shocking news.

During the investigation, detectives discovered an audio tape of three men planning the attack. Jeff Goillooly—the ex-husband of skater Tonya Harding, Shawn Eckhardt—Harding's bodyguard, and Shane Stant—the man who attacked Nancy. All three were found guilty of the crime. Why did they do it? They wanted to take Nancy out of the competition. Then their friend Tonya Harding would have a better chance to make the Olympic team.

Tonya did skate well and won the U.S. Nationals, making the Olympic team. In the weeks that followed, newspapers, magazines and TV reports were filled with the question: Was Tonya Harding involved in the attack on Nancy Kerrigan?

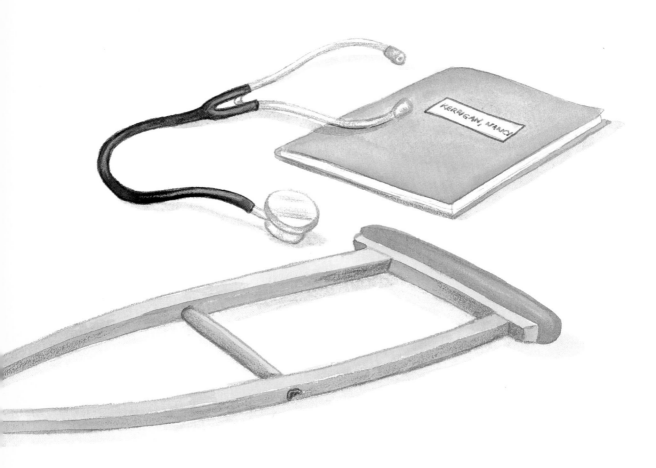

Fighting Back

United States skating officials promised Nancy that if she could get back in shape from her knee injury by February 6, she would be on the Olympic team. So, under a doctor's watchful eye, Nancy began to exercise and train. She fought hard and soon was on her way to a courageous recovery.

Nancy showed the world she was back during a skating exhibition for TV called *Nancy Kerrigan and Friends.* Nancy was the featured skater and she performed beautifully. The event raised money for several charities.

The 1994 Olympics took place in Lillehammer, Norway. The world was glued to their TV sets as Nancy Kerrigan once again stepped onto the ice. As she began to skate, something magical happened. Never before had she skated so flawlessly. When she finished her routine, the crowd gave her a standing ovation and Nancy smiled proudly. America smiled back at Nancy. She not only brought home the silver Olympic medal, but was a shining example of courage, too!

"I am Nancy's biggest fan," says her mom. "She is not only a beautiful skater but a beautiful person as well. She will always be my closest friend."

Nancy

KERRIGAN

TIMELINE AND TRIUMPHS

1969   Born October 13, in Woburn, Massachusetts

1990   Eastern Senior Championships—1st place

1990   U.S. Olympic Festival—1st place

1991   Eastern Senior Championships—1st place

1991   Nations Cup—1st place

1992   National Senior Championships—2nd place

1992   Olympic Winter Games—3rd place
       (bronze medal)

1992 World Championships—2nd place

1992 Chrysler Concorde Pro-Am Challenge—
1st place

1993 National Senior Championships—1st place

1993 Piruetten Championships—1st place

1993 AT&T Pro–Am Challenge—1st place

1994 Olympic Winter Games—2nd place
(silver medal)

GREAT COMEBACK CHAMPIONS

ARTHUR ASHE
Tennis Legend

BO JACKSON
Super Athlete

JOE MONTANA
The Comeback Kid

JULIE KRONE
Fearless Jockey

MUHAMMAD ALI
The Greatest

NANCY KERRIGAN
Courageous Skater